I0481533

Blockchain:

Everything You Need to Know

About the Technology Behind

Cryptocurrency and Bitcoin

Mark Clarkson

Table of Contents

Introduction

Congratulations on purchasing *Blockchain: Everything You Need to Know About the Technology Behind Cryptocurrency and Bitcoin* and thank you for doing so. While you may not understand the specifics behind blockchain technology, you have no doubt heard of Bitcoin, the investor darling that blockchain technology made possible. While Bitcoin is by far the most famous example of the technology, it is far from the extent of what blockchain can do. Learning the ins and outs of this new technology can put you in a unique position to take advantage of what is being called the most important new technology since the creation of the internet.

Like any new technology, however, it can be a bit confusing for the uninitiated. As such, the following chapters will discuss everything you ever wanted to know about blockchain technology and how you can put it to use for you. First, you will learn the basics of what makes the technology tick. Then, you will learn more about cryptocurrency, blockchain's most famous creation. Next, you will learn about the pros and cons of investing in blockchain technology for your business.

From there, you will learn about the ways blockchain technology is likely to affect business of all types in the coming years. You will also learn about various blockchain companies that are worth keeping an eye on. Finally, you will learn what 2018 and beyond likely holds for this amazing new technology.

There are plenty of books on this subject on the market, thanks again for choosing this one! Every effort was made to ensure it is full of as much useful information as possible, please enjoy!

Chapter 1: Blockchain Basics

By the start of 2018, it is unlikely that you are completely unfamiliar with the concept of cryptocurrency, which means you have likely heard the term blockchain at least once or twice. If you still aren't really sure what it's all about, don't worry. You aren't alone, as only about half the population can accurately describe both terms, and a far smaller amount actually puts one or both to use on a regular basis. As you might have deduced from the name, blockchains are a type of digital ledger that stores blocks of data in an interconnected fashion.

New data is added to a blockchain from one of a theoretically limitless number of nodes that a blockchain can support. As the digital ledger is also decentralized, these nodes can be located anywhere in the world. Being decentralized also means that there does not need to be a single controlling force telling the blockchain how to operate; it will go through the motions of taking in data, offloading the verification process, adding new blocks to the chain, and updating the nodes with the newest version of the chain, all automatically.

Aside from storing a wide variety of different types of data, each block also includes a timestamp in reference to its generation, along with other classification data to ensure the chain easily knows how to sort it. This is only one of the ways in which blockchain technology promotes automation and ensures its decentralized nature never needs to be compromised.

Blockchain offers up the almost unprecedented ability to allow users access to their own transactions, while at the same time ensuring that all of the data in the blockchain remains both secure and immutable. If a transaction then ends up not matching what the chain expects, either when the block is first added to the chain or at a later point, it is automatically deleted and replaced with an earlier, already verified, version of the corrupted data (if applicable).

Additionally, if, somehow a block is added that includes false data, it will still be detected, as 51 percent of all the currently active nodes have to sign off on the logical legitimacy of the new block before it will be accepted permanently into the blockchain as a whole.

While this security protocol makes blockchain technology virtually tamperproof these days, as the cost of creating enough nodes to hijack an entire blockchain wouldn't be worth the payout, this may not always be the case. The way to successfully crack blockchain's security is well-known; it is just a matter of someone coming along who is able to execute on it.

Simple Beginnings

The first aspect of blockchain technology to come into existence is the proof of work model that is currently used to verify every block in the blockchain prior to its being added to the blockchain proper, in a process that is often referred to as mining. The proof of work model was created in the early 1990s to deal with a new and dangerous problem, email spam. When built into an email client, the proof of work model would require the sender's program to complete a complicated equation to send the email successfully. While sending an email to a few people at a time would be no big deal, sending that email to a thousand people, or more, at once proved to be more than the computers of the day could handle.

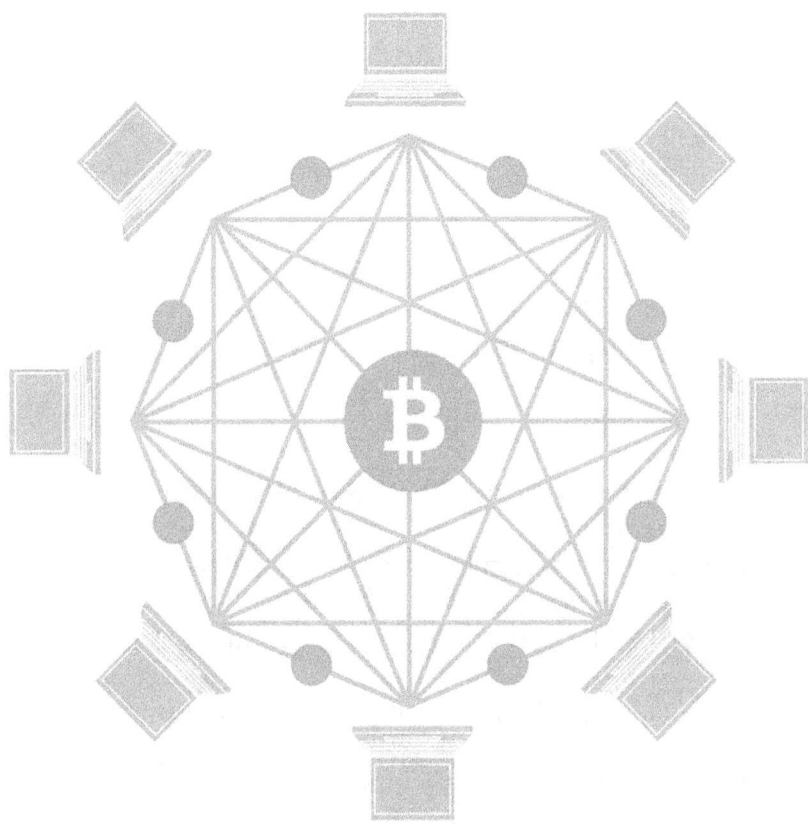

Despite its use, this technology never really caught on and more or less lay fallow for more than a decade. At that point, it was late 2008, and a number of programmers were having a discussion on a P2P programming forum about the

likelihood of a digital currency coming along and replacing
fiat currency. While most of the programmers considered the
conversation to be little more than a thought experiment,
one person, using the alias Satoshi Nakamoto, felt
differently.

In October 2008, he returned to the forum with a treatise
outlining the purpose and philosophical guidelines behind
Bitcoin, along with the opensource code for both blockchain
technology in general, and the Bitcoin blockchain
specifically. From there, Nakamoto distributed bitcoins to a
number of the other programmers on the site, before mining
the first block and setting the entire blockchain in motion.
From there, it didn't take long before other programmers
expressed interest in the project and the Nakamoto alias
faded into the background. Rumors persist, however, that
the alias also left a Bitcoin wallet behind that, by now, would

be enough to make anyone who found it a billionaire overnight.

Parts of a blockchain

Database:

The biggest difference between a blockchain database and a traditional database is the level of centralization required for it to function as intended. With a centralized database, the goal is to ensure the servers remain as close to one another as possible to ensure that data is transferred with utmost efficiency. On the other hand, decentralized databases give up on this desire for speed in exchange for the added utility related to a database that can be accessed with the same ease from anywhere in the world.

When this flexibility is combined with the unique aspects of blockchain's security, which ensure information isn't going anywhere once it gets in, and its ability to easily sort blocks regardless of where they are coming from, you get a revolutionary new banking system that is not only secure but autonomous and independent as well. You can think of a blockchain transferring currency in the same way the internet transmits information.

Hashes:

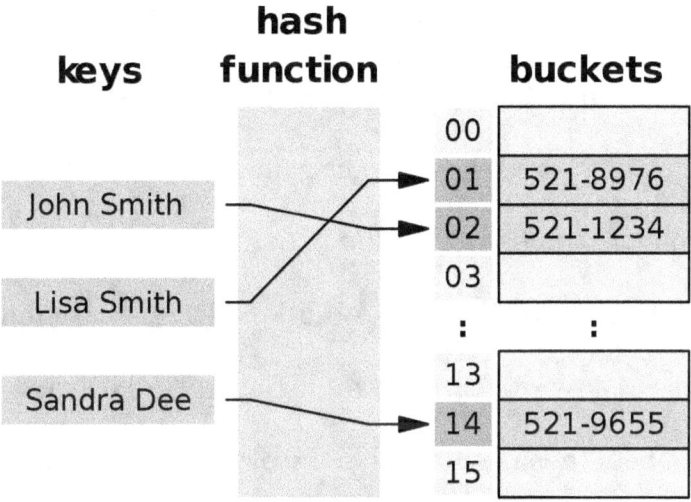

The data that is stored in each block of a blockchain can neatly be broken into two types, the data the block was created to store, and the data about the block itself. A large amount of this data is then going to naturally concern the data that users add to the chain or the cryptocurrency transactions that take place in association with one cryptocurrency or the other. When a block is full and ready to be added to a blockchain, it needs to be verified by a third party to ensure it is legitimate.

Once this is done, the block is then accepted into the blockchain, after being encrypted through a hash function. As such, even if a hacker illegally gains access to the blocks with your personal information in them, they would only be able to see the hash function. Additionally, this hash function operates as a type of cryptographic fingerprint, which means that if any of the information in the block is changed, the resulting hash will change, as well. The most commonly used hash amongst the blockchain community is the SHA256 hash.

Once a block is part of the blockchain, its hash is then added to the hash of those blocks around it, and so on and so forth, until the entire blockchain has its own unique hash, which is updated each time a new block is added to the chain. If the details for a block don't match those of the surrounding

blocks, then the new block won't make it into the chain.

Merkle tree:

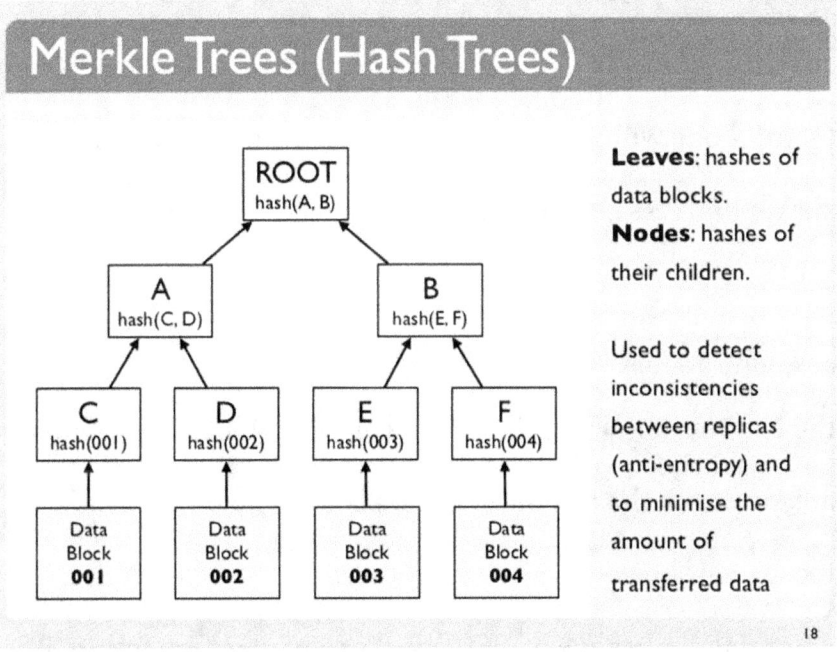

Merkle tree is the name given to a blockchain process that

ensures blockchains can run in a decentralized manner in the

first place. It is essentially a functionality matrix that allows

the blockchain to verify that everything is intact in the time between new blocks are added to the chain. It also makes it easier for vast financial transactions to be broken into chunks which are easier to digest, which makes it possible for users to follow the follow the flow of the trade data as easily as possible. The Merkle tree is also a critical part of the security protocols of the blockchain, and while it is possible to build one without the other, those versions tend to be slower and less secure than the preferred version.

The hash that is the sum total of all of the other hashes on the chain is known as the root hash. The Merkle tree is then able to check the root hash as it exists against the most recent root hash that was officially verified, to determine potential discrepancies. If these discrepancies are found, it then forks its process and continues checking the blockchain as it is, along with the blockchain as it believes it should be, to ensure that the overall process is not slowed while the issue in question is dealt with.

Manually verifying this amount of data would be a colossal task that, if performed by people, would make blockchain transactions an impossibility. The Merkle tree simplifies this process and also limits the amount of data that individual nodes would need to share at any given time, which speeds up the process even more. Every time that a particular hash is flagged in multiple locations, it is checked and double checked for accuracy across corresponding nodes.

Chapter 2: Blockchain and Cryptocurrency

While blockchain is poised to do a great many different things in the near future, for now, the most important thing you will want to keep in mind is that blockchains make cryptocurrency possible. Bitcoin jumped in price to more than $19,000 during 2017. While this price has pushed it out of the league of many amateur investors, there are more than 1,000 different cryptocurrencies on the market these days, so there are plenty of opportunities out there for those who are interested in a potentially profitable investment. This is not to say that there isn't risk involved as well, however; it is important to keep the risks of cryptocurrency investment in mind as well before making any investments in the space.

Here are the advantages and disadvantages of cryptocurrencies:

Pros

Lower likelihood of fraud:

As cryptocurrencies are an all-digital currency, this means there is less likelihood of fraud taking place around them;

they cannot be counterfeited, and there is no way for the one member of the transaction to reverse it once a transaction has taken place.

Less chance of identity theft:

Once you have bought into a cryptocurrency, there is less chance that you will have to worry about identity theft than when working with traditional online exchanges. This is a concern in traditional instances, as credit or debit cards are charged with each new transaction, which means that there is a far greater opportunity for identity thieves to find a way to crack the system and make off with personal information.

Extreme access:

Currently, there are three billion people in the world who have access to the internet but do not have regular access to any form of exchange. This leaves the cryptocurrency market with a lot of room to maneuver, and it is expected to see significant growth as it gains wider acceptance. This means that an increasing amount of business will take place purely through digital currencies, which means those who invest in cryptocurrency now aren't just likely to see an increase; they are likely to see a dramatic increase. For example, as of 2017, fifty percent of all Kenyans now own a Bitcoin wallet, while less than forty percent have access to reliably clean water and only thirty percent have modern plumbing.

Less cost:

Despite the fact that every cryptocurrency transaction comes with an accompanying transaction fee, the fees for utilizing a cryptocurrency exchange are almost always going to be lower than what the traders who use more traditional exchanges pay on a regular basis.

Cons

Uncertain future:

While Bitcoin has proved to be a winning investment for the past eight years, and Ethereum has grown year over year since its inception, despite some down times in-between, that doesn't mean that this will continue to be the case in the long-term. There simply isn't enough past data to say with any real degree of certainty what the market will look like a year from now, much less 5 or 10, which means that both the potential for loss and the potential for gain are virtually limitless. Basically, what this means is that up until the time that the cryptocurrency market stabilizes, any dollar you put into Ethereum is just as likely to be worth more next year than it is today as it is to be completely worthless.

Extremely volatile:

While bitcoin can be thought of as the most stable cryptocurrency, it is still six times as volatile than investing in the S&P 500 and five times as volatile as investing in gold. While this means there is an increased chance of profit, it also means there is an increased chance for risk as well. A vast majority of all cryptocurrency transactions are currently speculative in nature, which means that investors are buying and holding them. This, in turn, creates a bubble that has to eventually burst sooner or later. The trick with the bubble is to get in as early as possible and keep an eye out for signs that it will burst so you can get while the getting is good.

Purely digital:

While the digital nature of cryptocurrency is often touted as a positive, it is important to consider its negative aspects as well. For example, as a purely digital construct, if you were keeping your cryptocurrency in an exchange that had a server error that resulted in a loss of all its backup drives, what would happen to your currency then? Likewise, what were to happen if you put your coins into a physical wallet that then stopped reading on your computer?

Both of these cases are unlikely to happen, but if they were, then your cryptocurrency would be gone as if it had never existed in the first place. Furthermore, the massive potential for profits means that hackers are never going to stop trying to access these exchanges, so eventually, they will succeed. When investing in cryptocurrency, it is important to value security as highly as possible because there is very little standing between your investments and the void.

Benefits to Trading in Cryptocurrency

Global currency:

When it comes to standard currency, the number of things that can influence the price is naturally going to be fairly limited. The opposite is true for cryptocurrencies, however, and it is difficult to tell what will set investors off before it happens. Any currency news anywhere has the potential to set prices shifting dramatically; in fact, several of Bitcoin's most significant moves have come about due to the introduction of controls for capital in Greece and when China devalued the Yuan.

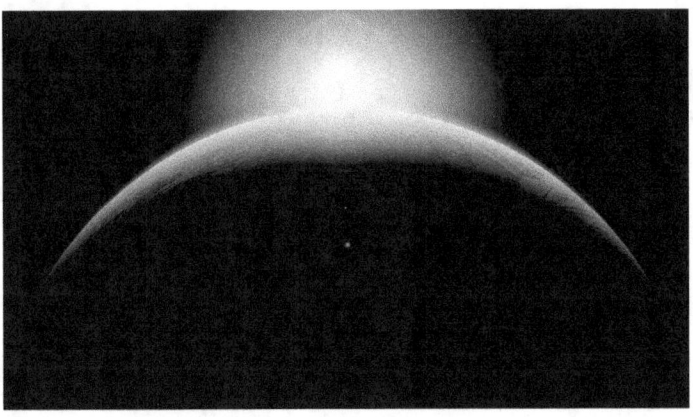

Market always ready:

While the Forex market is traditionally thought of as the most robust market, as it is open 120 hours each week, the cryptocurrency market is open 168 hours each week, and trades are always happening regardless of what part of the world is currently active. Currently, there are about 100 major cryptocurrency exchanges in the world who all offer various levels of trading, along with differing rates based on their level of service. As such, it should not take more than a little research to find the one that is right for you.

This can also be seen as a negative, depending on your tolerance for risk, as these factors can be enough to generate large swings on a daily basis. In fact, price shifts of more than 5 percent are common on most days for the larger cryptocurrencies, and the smaller ones aren't surprised if they see 15 percent movement or more.

High volatility:

The fact that cryptocurrencies are not regulated by any higher power, coupled with the fact that they are a new form of investment and the fact that any event anywhere can lead to essentially unexpected movement, all combine to create an extremely volatile market. Swings of more than 5 percent in a single day are not uncommon for several different types of cryptocurrency, and the smaller currencies are capable of swinging with even greater frequency and to larger degrees.

A Note on the Ethereum Platform

Of all the cryptocurrencies on the market today, the one that is the most dedicated to improving the quality of the blockchain experience as a whole is Ethereum. While its cryptocurrency, ether, sees a fair amount of speculation, it is mainly used to pay for transactions with smart contracts and

applications designed to run on the Ethereum platform. It

has already seen about half as many transactions as Bitcoin,

despite only being around for a third of the time. It is also

more firmly focused on the future, with its improved

interactions with smart contracts and its decentralized app

platform, as well.

Perhaps more importantly, if you look at the transaction

chart for Bitcoin, then you will see that it is nothing but

peaks and valleys. It's true that things tend to move in an

overall positive direction, but it can hardly be called steady

growth.

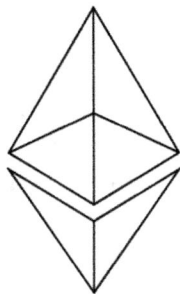

On the contrary, the Ethereum chart shows a much more overall bullish outlook, even through the summer of 2017, when blockchain was at its current peak. It is important to keep in mind that cryptocurrencies are always going to be social constructs, which means that Ethereum's robust network effects make it easier for the network, and its value, to continue to grow steadily moving forward.

The final feather in ether's cap is the fact that the Ethereum blockchain is all done on smart contract technology. Smart contracts are simple programs that can be added to blocks and then activated once a specific set of circumstances occur. While they are currently primarily being used for financial purposes, there is already interest in them for everything from monitoring patients in hospitals to providing notary services. In fact, one of the stated goals of Ethereum is to simplify the way that traditional contracts work, thus reducing the costs of such services significantly.

The Ethereum platform can process a total of 25 transactions per second, though additional scalability is also possible. This process can lead to additional orphaned blocks that are never processed correctly; however, this isn't an especially common occurrence. As of November 2017, a single ether is worth about $350. By January, it was above $900.

Chapter 3: Understanding Blockchain

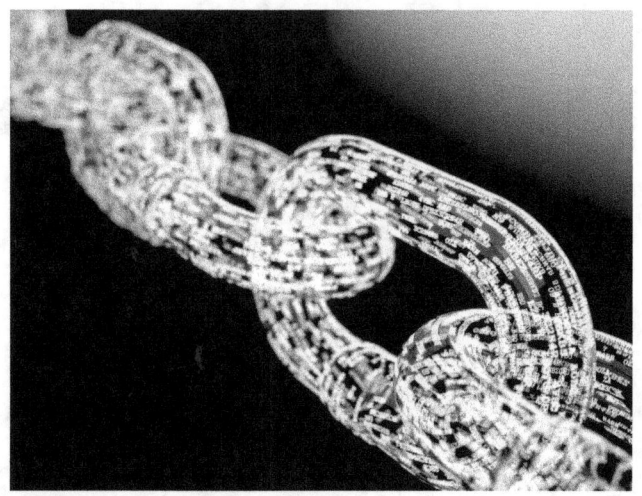

If you like what you have heard so far, then you are likely interested in experimenting a little with blockchain as a way of determining if it is the right course of action for you and your company. The most common reasons that people typically consider experimenting with blockchain is an ongoing desire to experiment with new technologies, a need for blockchain's timestamp technology, or an interest in the many ways blockchain can safeguard existing data. However, it is important to look before you leap. That said, consider the following to see if blockchain is really for you.

First and foremost, you must ensure that you have the right expectations when it comes to what blockchain technology can do for you. It is not some type of miracle cure that is good for fixing whatever is currently ailing your company. Rather, it is good for dealing with a variety of very specific issues, but only if you know what you are trying to do with it first; it's not something you can decide after it is up and running.

Understand who will have access to the data:

When it comes to centralized databases, anyone with access to the database has their activities stored in case a review is required at a later date. If you need to give lots of users read-only access to your data and don't want to worry about having to limit them from write access, then a blockchain can easily streamline this process. You can set the blockchain to be viewable in a non-hash format and still log access in a more traditional way if it is required.

High Costs:

While it is true that the distributed nature of a blockchain is what makes them so useful when preventing fraud, it also makes them extremely inefficient. When it comes to the cost of all of the additional computer resources as well as the electricity that these resources consume, the cost is enough to be prohibitive in numerous scenarios. For example, the estimated costs of each confirmed Bitcoin transaction is said to be at roughly what it would cost to run the average household for 36 hours. This is not something that is likely to decrease either, as the distributed nature of the process is one of its most lauded features. As such, it is important that you keep in mind exactly what kind of benefit you are getting

out of blockchain technology before diving in too deep.

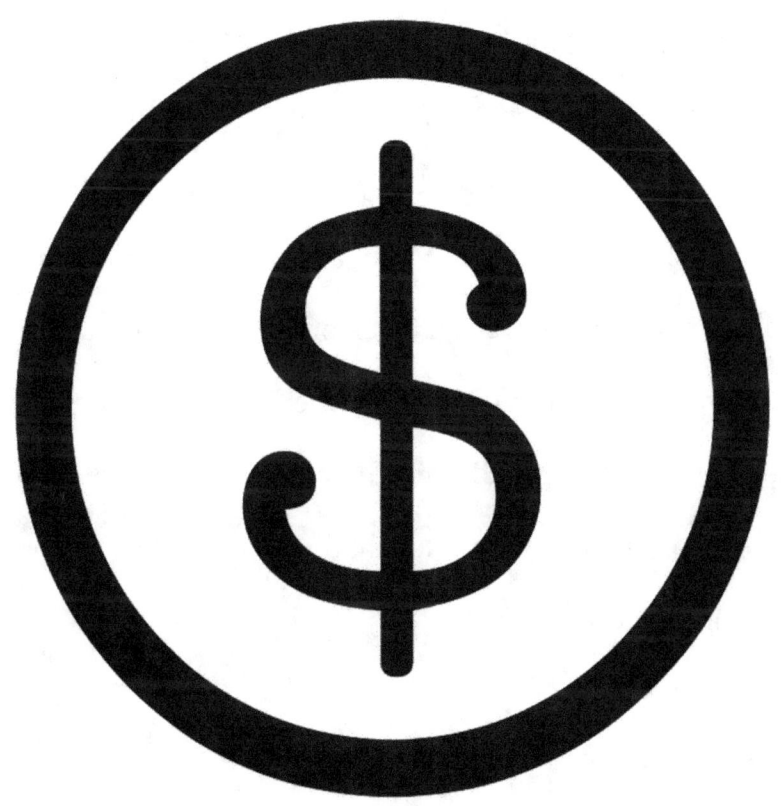

Read data:

When it comes to most centralized databases, knowing who accesses what is typically stored in a different location or set of log files. If you are looking for a way to streamline this process, depending on its settings, a blockchain can be read without actually accessing it from a database node. Once changes are made to a given block or chain, those changes are then stored in a traditional log file. If you have files that need to be secured but also need them to be regularly seen by those who can look but not touch, then a blockchain is a preferable solution.

Writing data:

When it comes to access, most centralized databases tend to be protected by a username- and password-based combination system, as well as various other authentication parameters for extremely secure scenarios. On the other hand, blockchains are secured via a digital signature as well as the aforementioned security. This comes into play when data is added to the blockchain at the block level, as well as each time a transaction is added to the chain, making it extremely clear where each transaction came from and who initiated it.

Functionally, what this means is that every time a transaction is completed, each participant has to digitally sign and confirm each transaction. However, it is possible to skip this step by adding information to a node indirectly instead. Additionally, when a block is added, another signature is required by the verifier before the block is added to the chain. Even if direct identification is not required, the IP address of everyone who interacts with a block is always recorded.

Changing data:

 One of blockchain's biggest strengths is that once data has been added to the blockchain, it is very difficult to change. If your business requires that you change data that has already been added to the database, you may want to consider sticking with more traditional databases for now. Essentially, the only way to change information that has already been added to the blockchain is to change it simultaneously across all the nodes where that information is already stored so that the chain doesn't mistake the change for a discrepancy and wipe it out before it can be saved. This can be quite resource-intensive depending on the specifics, which automatically disqualifies blockchain for everyday use in many situations.

Backing up data:

When it comes to direct comparisons to more traditional

types of databases, backing up data may be the area where blockchain technology will save the most time. While more traditional databases require specific user authorization when it comes to backups and updates, decentralized databases automate all of these functions. Remember, each time a new block is added to the blockchain, it is spread across every node in the system. This means that a new backup is created every time, automatically. What's more, as long as all of the nodes on the system don't end up going down at exactly the same time, it is virtually impossible for all the data to be lost.

This, then, makes the decentralized database a terrific choice for users who are looking to store sensitive information that many people need to see, but few people need to touch. It will ensure that the data remains securely ensconced in the blockchain, no matter what. Depending on the costs that are currently being dedicated to backing up existing information, the costs associated with creating a decentralized database could be offset significantly.

Location specific data:

While it is likely not going to be an issue most of the time, the fact is that it is impossible to limit the location of the data in the blockchain to a specific node, without updating that node specifically and then manually detaching it from the network. Even then, when it was reconnected, the data would be spread to the other nodes. As such, if you will need to keep data within certain geographic bounds, whatever the reason, then it is likely that a blockchain database isn't for you.

Interoperability:

Another way in which blockchain technology streamlines business processes is by allowing multiple blockchains to interact with one another for specified periods of time. This makes it quite simple to provide external access to those who may need to connect to your data for just a single project, without having to worry about updating security protocols when their project is complete. This provides for the possibility of a wide variety of secondary options that centralized databases simply aren't equipped to deal with, including automating even more processes, thanks to smart contracts. The downside to this type of functionality is that giving someone access to your blockchain gives them access to the entire blockchain, so extremely secure data should perhaps be stored on a secondary blockchain with limited access.

Amount of data stored:

When it comes to determining if a decentralized database is right for you, one of the more important factors to consider is the amount of data you plan on pushing through the system on a regular basis and how often you will be creating new blocks. The most effective blockchains are those that keep the amount of data transferred per block to a minimum, as transferring large amounts of data with every block can end up slowing the entire blockchain down significantly. This means that if you are hoping to move gigs and gigs of data, per day, then a more traditional database might better suit your needs. Additionally, the write speed of a centralized database will be much faster as well, making it the clear choice if speed is of the essence.

Validation:

While the proof of work model that cryptocurrencies use to validate their blocks will likely be a little bit excessive for your blockchain's needs, you are still going to need to use some type of validation system for your blockchain to function properly. Depending on the size and scope of your blockchain, the easiest thing to do is to have users take turns validating transactions after they take place. Likewise, if you will open your blockchain up to the public, for whatever reason, then using third party validators is always an option; however, you would need to consider how you will compensate them for their time if you go down this route.

Chapter 4: Blockchain and Business

It is common for many businesses, but specifically small businesses, to feel trapped by their relationship with their local bank. Using a bank has always been a requirement, since there were no other ways to verify a variety of transactions. But the fact remains: banking practices rarely go out of their way to favor business owners. Unfortunately, with the way that society operates, there were few, if any, alternatives traditionally available, outside of saying screw it and only accepting cash, hardly a viable solution in the age of online shopping.

Luckily, businesses that take the time to find out more details regarding blockchain technology will often find that not only are the prices more reasonable, but it also comes with a wide variety of additional benefits as well. What's more, the fact that cryptocurrencies can easily be used anywhere in the world means that adopting this technology naturally leads to an increase in potential customers as well.

What's more, the distributed ledger nature of the technology not only allows for access to the data at the most granular level, but it also allows for unprecedented levels of security on par with anything that a third party would be able to provide. It also allows business owners to remain completely in charge of their own data, further minimizing the risk of a wide variety of cybersecurity attacks. This is another natural benefit of the technology, as it is much easier to attack large stores of data rather than small pockets.

Each time a transaction processes through the blockchain, a fee is charged; this fee is split between the miner of the transaction and the blockchain itself for maintenance fees. Despite this fact, these fees remain, by and large, far cheaper than what a bank charges for similar services. Given the number of transactions that the average business generates per month, the savings in this avenue could be substantial.

Furthermore, dealing with transactions that are already connected to the blockchain is far easier when it comes to things like clearing or settling existing bank transactions. While these processes can traditionally take a few days or more using traditional financial services, this same level of transaction validation is available on the average blockchain in minutes, if not seconds. Almost unilaterally, cryptocurrency transactions will be verified before their fiat cousins, especially if the transaction takes place on the weekend.

Even better, when these benefits are combined with the potential that smart contract technology has to reshape business as we know it, the possibilities associated with streamlining process and automation become virtually endless. While some of these businesses will naturally be outside the scope of smaller businesses, the cost of implementing such features is only going to decrease as standard blockchain functionality becomes more commonplace. Given a timeframe of even five years, blockchain technology is virtually guaranteed to affect small business of all types, helping them to run more efficiently, while also reducing operating costs across the board.

A large part of this streamlining process is sure to come about – thanks to the ease with which the technology will handle dealing with contracts of all types. Due to the fact that a vast majority of all business involves transferring value between at least two parties, the most common blockchain usage scenario is likely going to be one that takes advantage of the most secure environment for doing so (the blockchain). What's more, any contract that taps into the power of blockchain technology can virtually automatically ensure that all of its conditional statements are properly followed through on by attaching them to smart contracts that are virtually guaranteed to be followed through on, assuming the proper triggering factors are met.

This potent combination of contracts and code is unique in that it allows all the involved parties in a given business transaction to operate with absolute faith in the system, and therefore the other parties in the transaction as well. This level of faith will improve business relationships across the board, with subcontractors as well as vendors, at all levels of production. It will also help to cut down on legal fees, as much of the red tape that lawyers exist to cut through will be naturally taken care of by blockchain and smart contract technology.

Implementation Considerations

When it comes to implementing blockchain technology successfully in your company, the first thing you will want to do is ensure that you approach the problem with the goal of strengthening your company's core competencies, as opposed to using blockchain technology as an excuse to pivot in an entirely new direction. Remember, the technology as a whole is still quite new, and betting the farm on some niche aspect of the technology is likely not the way to go.

Instead, it is important that you look for ways to invest in the technology that will allow you to approach it in a strategic way that will work with what the company is already best at, in an effort to make things even better still. The best way to go about doing so will be getting a group of individuals together who can tackle the problem directly, though one of them should be in charge of making sure that things don't get too far out of hand and that any proposed innovation actually has the company's best interests at heart. This is crucial, as it is easy for these groups to get so caught up in their new technology that they try and shove it into as many different places as they can, as opposed to focusing on those that would naturally benefit the most.

To ensure that things proceed productively from the beginning, the first thing this group should focus on is blockchain-based projects that will generate the most visible amount of benefit for the smallest overall cost. Not only will moving forward with this type of project help the company explore blockchain technology without breaking the bank, if it is successful it will serve as a natural poster child for additional growth in this area.

When it comes to choosing the best project to start with, the best place to look for ideas will be natural pain points that the company has traditionally had a hard time solving. This should hopefully allow for a replacement to a commonly accepted workaround or the mitigation of an ongoing customer issue.

While having this list is a great place to start, it is equally important that the group gather insight from all of the relevant shareholders in the company to ensure that the project that is selected will do the most good for the most people. There is likely only going to be one test of the cryptocurrency technology; after all, it is best to make it count. Common suggestions for this project will be things that generate the greatest amount of disruption to the status quo, or those that follow the trends of the moment. It is important to maintain focus, keep the big picture in mind, and understand that institutional change does not happen overnight.

This should, in turn, make it easier for the group to focus in on the projects that will be the most good, in the shortest period of time, for the most reasonable cost. Ideally, this will include ways in which they can help the company outpace the competition or to otherwise generate proof that blockchain technology is worth backing more aggressively in the future.

Once the group knows how they should best move forward, the next thing they will need to do is put their concept into action on a small scale through the implementation of a prototype. The parameters of the prototype can change over time as new parameters are explored, but it is important that someone remains the voice of reason to ensure that things don't stray so far from the goal that the entire point of the project is called into question.

During this phase, it is also important to pay careful attention to the deadlines that the project is given, as they should be strict enough that the right amount of effort be applied, though not so rigid that experimentation is not possible. Above all else, of course, it is important that deadlines continue to remain relevant and that the project continually moves towards completion.

When it comes to rolling out the technology on a larger scale, however, it is important to keep in mind that fully implementing a blockchain on even a minimal scale is a long-term proposition. This means that your early goals should stick to things such as improving compliance, reducing costs, improving overall quality cost reductions, and the like. After this, then you can get buy-in on them from all the relevant parties. A unified approach will make it easier to create an implementation and scaling roadmap that actually has a chance of being followed.

Chapter 5: Blockchain Companies to Watch

There is plenty about blockchain technology to be interested in moving forward, and the potential for profit is certainly among them. What follows is a list of blockchain companies that are already making the world a better place, while making their investors a serious profit in the process.

Cloud storage:

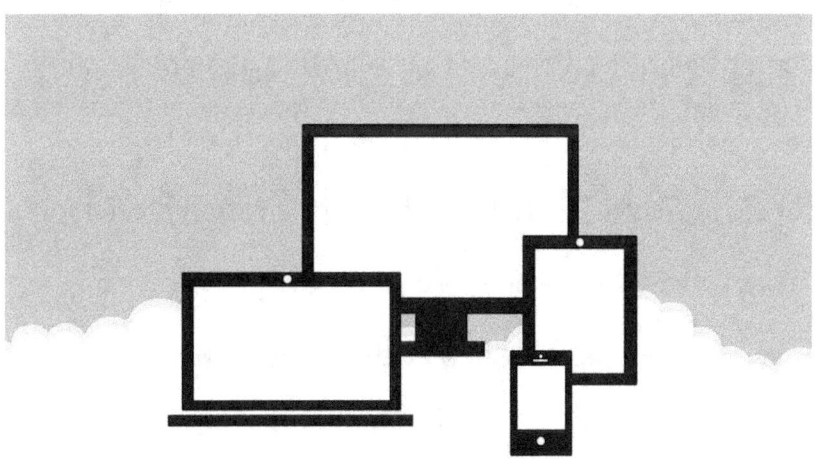

Studies show that the average PC has at least 100 gigabytes of hard drive space that is being underutilized, and that the average business that is paying for traditional cloud storage has a dozen terabytes or more of unused space within their walls. Companies such as Storj Labs are working to allow users to take full advantage of their hard drive space, or rent the extra storage space they need at a fraction of the cost of what more traditional cloud storage companies charge.

As such, the Storj app takes advantage of the innate blockchain security to ensure that the files are stored securely, while at the same time allowing them to remain easily accessible as well. Functionally, Storj works as a sort of storage marketplace that connects those with the need for extra storage space with those with extra storage up for grabs. The P2P network in play then naturally connects the two much more quickly than a larger business would because it doesn't have to deal with the heavy load the larger company runs under. Furthermore, due to the fact that users are able to specify exactly how much storage they need, the costs they have to pay will prove to be more in line with the services they are receiving.

The way these types of services typically work is through extremely large datacenters that are both extremely expensive to set up and run, as the costs of the servers don't scale in a meaningful way. Naturally, then, these higher costs are then passed along to the consumer. Furthermore, compared to a large server farm, having data distributed across thousands of different individual systems means that it is much harder for hackers to track down anything useful to steal. Currently, Storj has nearly 30,000 users utilizing unused storage on more than 10,000 computers.

Online identity:

While having one username and password for all of the internet might sound like something out of a late-80s movie that didn't understand how the internet worked, the fact of the matter is that it is closer to reality than you might expect. The company SecureKey has partnered with IBM to work on an initiative that will promote this future on a worldwide level. When adopted in a significant way, this initiative will have the ability to connect government bureaucracies, healthcare providers, financial services, telecommunications companies, and more through one blockchain network that is equally accessible to all.

This blockchain is being constructed on the back of HyperLedger technology, which was created by the Linux Foundation to run on the IBM blockchain structure. Once it is fully up and running, it will make use of what is known as the distributed trust model, which makes it possible for users to specify which of these organizations has access to their data, going so far as to ask consent each time a new request for data is processed.

A pilot program for the technology is already well underway in Canada, with many of the country's leading banks, including TD Bank, Desjardins Group, Canadian Imperial Bank of Commerce, Scotia Bank, Royal Bank of Canada, and the Bank of Montreal all taking part in the program. The system is already stable enough to make it easily scalable when new companies jump on board; it is able to ensure that the level of functionality remains secure. As with cloud storage, the natural perks of blockchain technology come into play here to ensure the end result is an overall attractive package.

Smart contracts:

While the level of excitement around smart contracts is still growing, rest assured that you will hear plenty more about them in the coming years. The Ethereum platform is already heavily invested in the technology, and it is the second most popular cryptocurrency on the market today. In fact, it was created specifically with smart contract use in mind, and there are already countless decentralized applications that run on the platform that you can take advantage of right now.

Specifically, they are already proving useful to artists in multiple ways, the first of which is being provided by a company known as BlockPhase. Its application allows those working in the AR, VR or 360-degree video space to upload their content to ensure it is safe online. Once it is a part of the BlockPhase blockchain, the associated technology then searches for unauthorized uses of the content and then activates a smart contract if violations are found. The smart contracts send a cease and desist letter to the person using the content without permission. Automating this process allows artists to focus on the creation of new content rather than protecting what they have already created.

Another approach to dealing with pirate content online is ContentKid. This company is utilizing blockchain technology to mitigate the consumption of pirated content by giving users a wider variety of alternatives when it comes to paying for the content they are interested in viewing. ContentKid works by connecting users with the traditional streaming services of the day, not for restrictive monthly contracts, but based on the amount of time they actually plan on interacting with the service.

From a consumer end, ContentKid makes it easier to watch media from a wide variety of different services, all in one place. Once an account is created on the blockchain and funds are added to it, users are then able to watch content as they see fit, and the fees for watching are automatically deducted from the relevant account, as needed. The idea here is that being able to pay a small amount to watch a half hour of content is far more palatable than paying for a month of a streaming service.

Notaries:

Due to the fact that many of the core features of blockchain fall in line with the types of things that notary services traditionally offer, using one to improve the other is a natural extension of blockchain technology. There are already many different companies, including Stamped.io, offering these services online, without any of the hassle typically associated with these services.

Stamped.io takes advantage of blockchain technology to allow users to indicate the authenticity of a specific file before the transaction has been completed, from virtually any internet browser. When a file is verified in this fashion, it is then supplied with a timestamp from the blockchain itself.

This transaction is then stored in a block that is further verified using what is known as the SHA256 hash, which ensures the data is beyond reproach. This process can be used effectively for any type of file and makes it impossible to deny if a specific file was in the hands of a specific individual at a specific time.

While this will save a mild hassle in some countries, in others, such as India, where the amount of bureaucratic maneuvering required can be quite extreme, it will likely cut months off the requirements for some transactions. Along similar lines, the ease of use associated with this expression of the service will mark the first time millions of people around the world have access to these types of services.

Voting:

The issues that the United States has experienced surrounding its elections in the twenty-first century have shown beyond a shadow of a doubt that the way elections are handled could use a modern update. Blockchain technology could be just what the process has been waiting for. The reasons for doing so are myriad, starting with the added security it would bring to the process and the fact that every vote would be automatically verified to ensure its validity before it is added to the blockchain. Each voter would also be able to verify their vote themselves, and even change it before the end of the election if they had a change of heart.

One company already making great strides in this arena is called Follow My Vote. Their system works with a series of specifically designed voting booths that record the personal details of voters before adding them to the Follow My Vote blockchain. Once they are a part of the system, voters will them be able to use the associated app to vote in any relevant elections and even watch the votes roll in in real time.

IoT:

IBM makes it on the list of blockchain superstars again, due to its work with blockchain and the internet of things. The internet of things allows a wide variety of internet-connected devices to communicate with one another for a wide variety of purposes. The Watson IoT platform is a scalable platform that was created to serve as a centralized hub for all the IoT needs of a modern business. The system also offers machine learning, image and text analytics, and natural language processing to make fulfilling the needs of the company as easy as possible.

Chapter 6: The Future of Blockchain Technology

Analyst reports from the end of 2017 place the current market capitalization for blockchain technology as a whole at around $410 million. These same reports estimate that this valuation will grow to more than $10 billion by 2022. This growth is primarily going to be driven by a rising demand for blockchain solutions across a wide variety of industries that are looking to improve their efficiency and speed in the ways that blockchain technology can facilitate.

Initially, financial transactions and various types of P2P payments will see the greatest amount of innovation first and foremost, with a majority of this growth anticipated to come from Asia. Noted consulting company Accenture further believes that 2018 will be the year that companies in this field stop considering their options and get ready to start moving into the adoption phase.

This is likely an accurate assessment, as a recent poll of major departmental leaders from 75 different financial institutions from around the world found that about half were already considering ways to put blockchain technology to use. Even better, a full 30 percent indicated that these plans would be up and running before the end of 2018. Cross-border remittances, digital identity management, clearing and settlement, letter of credit processes, and syndication of loans are the most likely candidates for commercial adoption.

Another interesting initiative in this sector is coming from Deutsche Bank UBS, Santander, and BNY Mellon. They recently announced their own cryptocurrency to be up and running by summer of 2018. According to the group, reliable, ready-to-run products across industries will have a positive business case within the next few years. Also of note is the cooperation between Bank of Tokyo-Mitsubishi UFJ (BTMU) and six other international banking groups, including Bank of America Merrill Lynch, Standard Chartered Bank of the U.K., Royal Bank of Scotland, Spain's Banco Santander, Canadian Imperial Bank of Commerce, and Australia's Westpac Banking. They will launch a faster and lower-cost cross-border wiring service that uses blockchain in 2018. US start-up Ripple will also continue to provide blockchain technology. This group will initially offer the global blockchain transfer service to individuals in early 2018, and then slowly expand to corporate clients.

While interest in this use case for the technology is already leading to highly publicized business deals, there is also an increasing interest in blockchain companies when it comes to traditional investment in the stocks of these companies. They are already representing a high growth potential, not on par with the speculative nature of cryptocurrency, but still robust for the stock market as a whole. At the same time, they are proving to be much more stable than the cryptocurrency option as well. Companies offering solutions for copyright verification and data management are already seeing solid returns and taking their early investors with them.

Along similar lines, about 20 percent of the world's leading health organizations are also anticipating having blockchain systems in place no later than 2020, with 2018 poised to see this number increase dramatically. Also in 2018, insurance provider AIG will roll out its first insurance contracts that are based around smart contract technology, making it possible for a vehicle that is internet-enabled to report the details of a crash Owners will have a claim paid out without an insurance adjuster getting involved at all. As soon as this rollout hits, it is likely that its competition will follow suit by 2020.

Due to these developments, it is estimated that roughly $5 billion worth of new investment will reach American fintech companies in 2018, with a large portion of that going towards blockchain companies directly. Industry trends also point to 2019 as the year that blockchain technology starts to become associated in the public's mind with more than just cryptocurrency, as more and more obvious use cases become readily available. This, in turn, will see usage double before the end of the year.

Aiding this level of growth will be the continued impressive speculative growth of cryptocurrencies of all shapes and sizes. While Bitcoin's price will continue to be out of reach of many who failed to invest early, many other cryptocurrencies will prove their worth, giving investors pause when it comes to the obvious choice for their investment dollars. Cryptocurrencies to keep an eye on include ripple, litecoin, ether, and lumens.

Government regulation

While there will be a lot of positive growth in the blockchain space in 2018, there is likely going to be a significant influx of new oversight before the year is out as well. Some level of oversight is to be welcomed, of course, as there are already countless stories out there of fraud, Ponzi schemes, and more surrounding the space. A safer public perception will ultimately help to fuel further investment in the space and help to get the technology to the point where it truly becomes mainstream.

The regulation that has been put into place thus far has all been based on avoiding penalties and playing catchup around companies that have unexpectedly found themselves at the top of the pile. As such, 2018 represents an opportunity for a new way forward to be established, one in which relevant community members are able to work with one another to develop standards that can be confidently held to moving forward. The best-case scenario for this type of leadership is a type of self-regulatory body akin to the ESRB, the video game ratings board which came into being when the industry felt pressure in the 1990s to regulate content that was not appropriate for everyone. While not a one to one comparison, it goes to show that only by working with lawmakers will the blockchain community be able to avoid regulations that do more harm than good.

The reason that some type of self-regulation in the industry is important is that the traditional lawmaking process is exceedingly slow. As such, the most common way for lawmakers to deal with new technology is to find a way to link it to an existing piece of legislation and issue hefty fines for those who step to close to the line. It goes without saying that this type of fiat lawmaking is not what the blockchain industry needs to thrive. True, rulemaking requires a careful examination of the issues, detailed inquiry into the ways that the market is developing and, perhaps most importantly, time to see how the market develops on its own.

As the snail's pace that effective lawmaking requires is nowhere near fast enough to keep up with the quick pace that blockchain technology is moving at, it makes 2018 the perfect time for the industry to start regulating itself. If this opportunity isn't seized on enthusiastically by members of the community, then the time for the community to lay down the law will pass, and companies will need to be content with whatever regulations governmental oversight sees fit to impose.

The best way to ensure that this is not the case is to see that a handful of public faces end up being attached to blockchain technology as a whole. While some leadership has already appeared in the space, it has largely been unexpected and accidental, but it is time for this process to stop being reactive and start being proactive.

Luckily, the Uniform Law Commission is currently working with members of the blockchain community to develop community standards that apply to cryptocurrency licensing in the hopes that they will be adopted nationwide. The SAFT project is currently working on something similar in the form of an opensource framework to enable practical and effective standards to codify token sales within the framework of existing laws.

Conclusion

Thank you for making it through to the end of *Blockchain: Everything You Need to Know About the Technology Behind Cryptocurrency and Bitcoin*. Let's hope it was informative and able to provide you with all of the tools you need to achieve your goals, whatever it is that they may be. Just because you've finished this book doesn't mean there is nothing left to learn on the topic; expanding your horizons is the only way to find the mastery you seek.

While it can be easy to get caught up in the unbridled promise that blockchain technology offers, it is important to not get so focused on the idea of utilizing blockchain technology at all costs that you fail to take into account the ways you can do so intelligently. Rushing headlong into the implementation phase will never do you any good, regardless of whether or not blockchain technology is the right decision for you and your company. Instead, it is important to take a more measured approach and ensure that when you do make a move, it is the right one. Remember, getting started with blockchain technology is a marathon, not a sprint. Slow and steady wins the race.

Your knowledge about blockchain and cryptocurrencies should not end here. Gather as much information as you to understand these advance technologies.

Finally, if you found this book useful in any way, a review on Amazon is always appreciated!

www.ingramcontent.com/pod-product-compliance
Lightning Source LLC
Chambersburg PA
CBHW071224220526
45468CB00002B/720